THE LIBRARY OF THE WESTERN HEMISPHERE™

Exploring COSTA RICA

with the FIVE Themes of Geography

by Amy Marcus

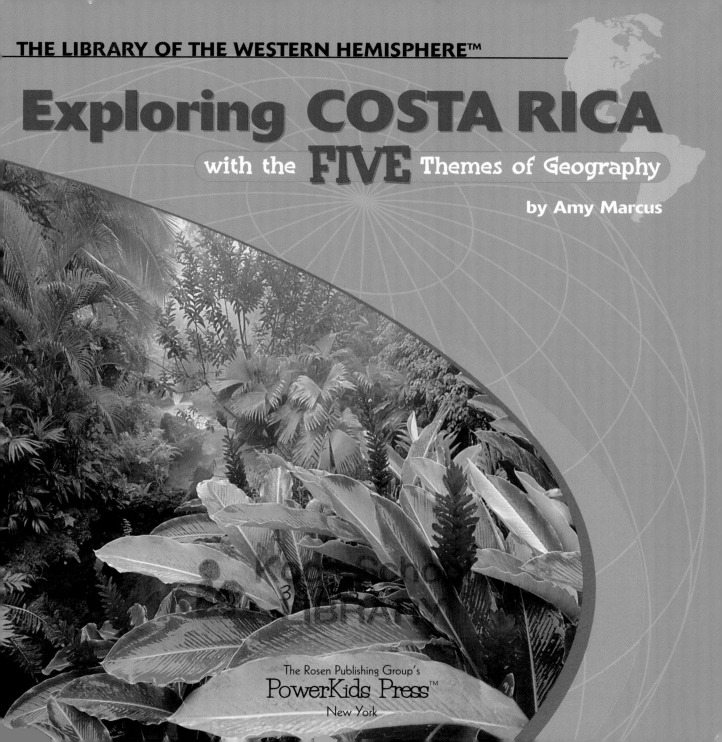

The Rosen Publishing Group's

PowerKids Press™

New York

Published in 2005 by The Rosen Publishing Group, Inc.
29 East 21st Street, New York, NY 10010

First Edition

Editor: Geeta Sobha
Book Design: Michelle Innes

Photo Credits: Cover, p. 1 © Chris Cheadle/Getty Images; p. 9 © Kevin Schafer/Corbis; p. 9 (wetlands) © Luke Hunter/Lonely Planet Images; p. 10 © Gay Bumgarner/Getty Images; p. 10 (frog) © George Grall/National Geographic Image Collection; p. 11 © Ralph Lee Hopkins/Lonely Planet Images; p. 12 © Photodisc/Getty Images; p. 12 (oxcart) © Wolfgang Kaehler/Corbis; p. 15 Tom Tracy/Getty Images; p. 15 (cloud forest) © Art Wolfe/Getty Images; p. 16 © Gary Braasch/Getty Images; p. 16 (San Jose) © Jose Fuste Raga/Corbis; p. 16 (logging truck) © Derek Hall, Frank Lane Picture Agency/Corbis; p. 19 © Frans Lemmens/Getty Images; p. 19 (bus) © Carl & Ann Purcell/Corbis; p. 19 (port) © Stephanie Maze/Corbis; p. 21 (waterfall) © Buddy Mays/Getty Images; p. 21 (shark) © Nikolas Konstantinou/Getty Images

Library of Congress Cataloging-in-Publication Data

Marcus, Amy.
    Exploring Costa Rica with the five themes of geography / by Amy
Marcus.— 1st ed.
    p. cm. — (The library of the Western Hemisphere)
    Includes bibliographical references (p.   ) and index.
    ISBN 1-4042-2672-9 (lib. bdg.) — ISBN 0-8239-4632-0 (pbk.)
    1. Costa Rica—Geography—Juvenile literature. [1. Costa
Rica—Geography.] I. Title. II. Series.

    F1543.9.M37 2005
    917.286—dc22
                                                    2003024543

Manufactured in the United States of America

Contents

Geography is the study of Earth, including its people, resources, climate, and physical features. When we study a particular country or area, such as Costa Rica, we use the five themes of geography: location, place, human-environment interaction, movement, and regions. By using these themes, we can organize and understand important information about the geography of places throughout the world. Let's see what the five themes can tell us about Costa Rica.

1 Location

Where is Costa Rica?

Costa Rica can be found by using its absolute, or exact, location. Absolute location tells exactly where a place is in the world. The imaginary lines of longitude and latitude are used to define the absolute location.

You can also define where Costa Rica is by using its relative, or general, location. Relative location describes where a place is by showing other places near it. Also, you can describe relative location by using the cardinal directions of east, west, north, and south.

2 Place

What is Costa Rica like?

To really know Costa Rica, we must study its physical and human features. The physical features include landforms, bodies of water, climate, natural resources, and plant and animal life. The human features, such as cities, buildings, government, and traditions, have been created by people.

3 Human-Environment Interaction

How do the people and the environment of Costa Rica affect each other?

Human-environment interaction explains how people adapt, or change to fit, the environment. It also explains how the environment has affected the way people live.

4 Movement

How do people, goods, and ideas get from place to place in Costa Rica?

Movement explains how products, people, and ideas move around the country. It can also show how they move from Costa Rica to other countries in the world.

5 Regions

What does Costa Rica have in common with other places around the world? How are places within Costa Rica grouped?

Places are grouped into regions by geographic and cultural features that they share. This theme shows features that Costa Rica shares with other areas to make it part of a certain region. Also, it explores geographic regions within Costa Rica.

Costa Rica's absolute location is 10° north and 84° west. You can define Costa Rica's relative location by looking at the places that surround it. Costa Rica is located in Central America. It is bordered on the north by the country of Nicaragua. On the southeastern border is the country of Panama. The Caribbean Sea lies at Costa Rica's east coast. The Pacific Ocean is on its west coast.

Where in the World?

Absolute location is the point where the lines of longitude and latitude meet.
Longitude tells a place's position in degrees east or west of the prime meridian, a line that runs through Greenwich, London.
Latitude tells a place's position in degrees north or south of the equator, the imaginary line that goes around the middle of the earth.

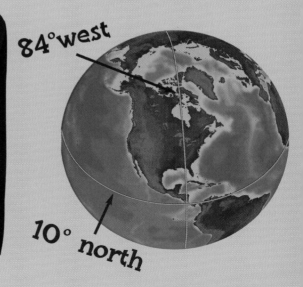

84°west

10° north

The capital of Costa Rica is San José, which is found in the middle of the Meseta Central.

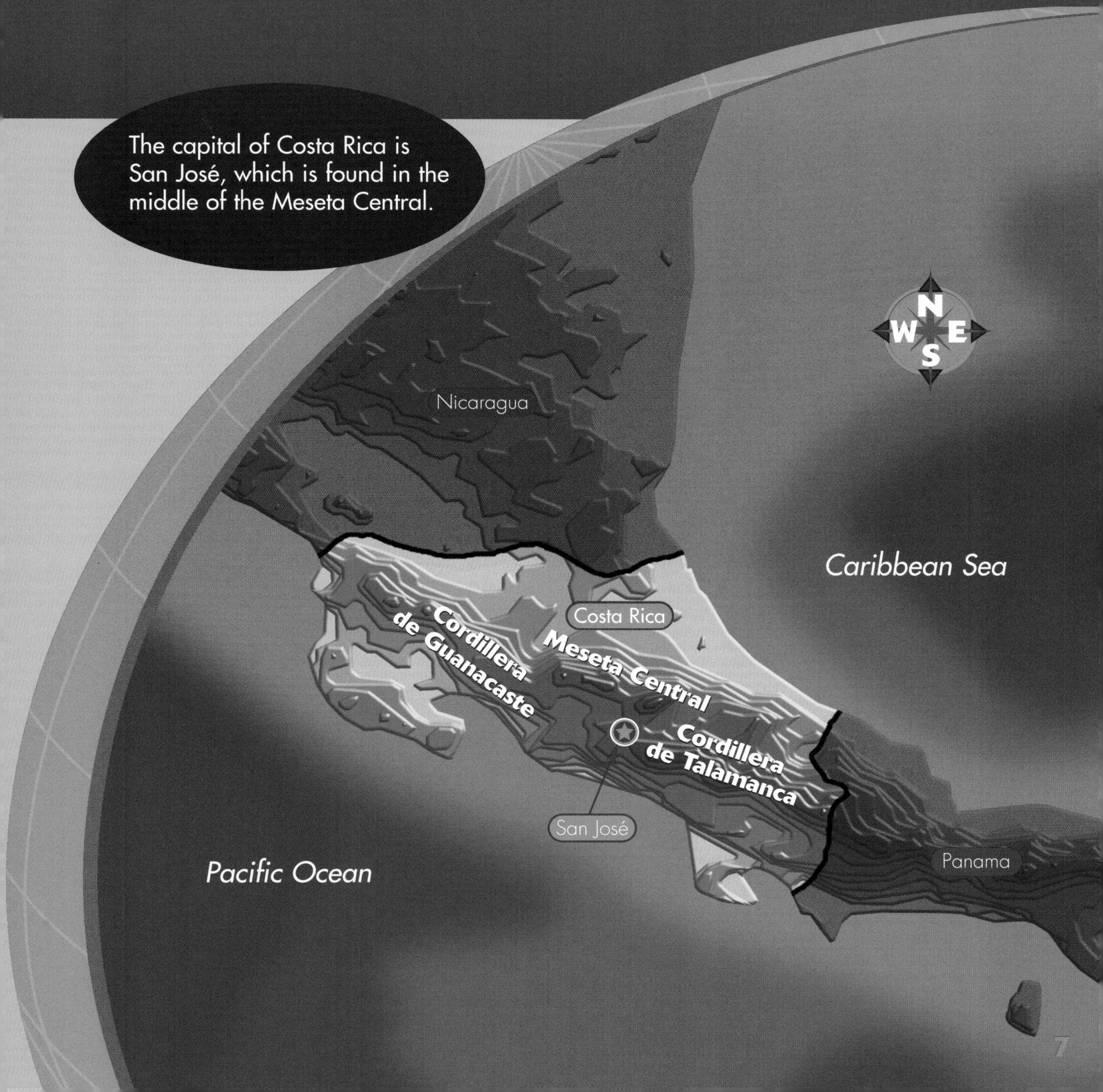

Nicaragua

Caribbean Sea

N
W · E
S

Costa Rica

Cordillera de Guanacaste

Meseta Central

Cordillera de Talamanca

San José

Pacific Ocean

Panama

Physical Features

Costa Rica is made up of many kinds of land. The Meseta Central, or Central Valley, is a large plateau with fertile farmland. The Reventazón River runs through the Meseta Central. The Caribbean lowlands lie along the east coast. The Pacific coastal strip is a hilly area along Costa Rica's west coast. Costa Rica is divided by two mountain chains: the Cordillera Volcánica and the Cordillera de Talamanca. There are more than 100 volcanoes in Costa Rica. Only a few of these volcanoes erupt regularly. The sand on some of Costa Rica's beaches is black, due to the volcanic rock along the shores.

Temperatures range from 75°F (24°C) in the highlands to 100°F (38°C) in the lowlands. Annual rainfall can range from 70 to 150 inches (178 to 381 centimeters)

Palo Verde National Park is located in northwestern Costa Rica. It has both dry forests and wetlands.

The Arenal Volcano first erupted in July 1968. Most recently it erupted in September 2003. Minor eruptions occur every hour, sending hot rocks and lava tumbling down its side.

Red eye tree frogs live in the rain forests of Costa Rica and other parts of Central America. It is believed that their red eyes are used to surprise attackers.

Leaf cutter ants can carry up to 10 times their weight.

per year in different parts of the country. Costa Rica also experiences hurricanes, which can cause great damage.

Three-toed sloths, many varieties of monkeys, green iguanas, marine turtles, pumas, and jaguars are among the wildlife found in Costa Rica. There are also colorful quetzals and hundreds of other types of birds.

One-third of Costa Rica's land is covered by forests of cedar, ebony, and mahogany trees. Palm trees grow along the Caribbean coast. There are also over 1,000 types of orchids, a flower that is native to Costa Rica.

The quetzal can be found in Costa Rica's rain forests. The males can grow tails more than three feet (.9 meters) long.

Costa Rica's colorfully decorated oxcarts have become symbols of the country.

The ruins of Costa Rica's oldest church, which was built in the 1500s, are in the city of Ujarras.

Human Features

Almost 3,900,000 people live in Costa Rica. About three-fourths of the people live in the Meseta Central. Most Costa Ricans are descended from Spanish settlers. Spanish is the official language. The native people of Costa Rica are known as Amerindians. Most Amerindians in Costa Rica are of the Bribrí and Cabécar peoples.

San José, Costa Rica's capital city, was settled in 1736. It is the center of government and politics. The architecture of San José's buildings ranges from modern high-rises to Spanish colonial styles. Most of the colonial buildings have been destroyed by earthquakes. Some of these have been restored.

Costa Rica is a democratic republic. The president serves as the nation's chief executive.

The Meseta Central of Costa Rica is the most populated area of the country. People of the Meseta Central rely on the rich soil and favorable climate as a means of producing many crops. However, farmers throughout the country grow crops, such as corn, rice, sugarcane, and cotton. Along the Caribbean lowlands, they grow bananas. Another resource for Costa Ricans is timber from the forests. Also, gold and silver are mined on the west coast, and salt is made from seawater.

Hydroelectric power is another important natural resource. It accounts for about 80 percent of the power in Costa Rica. Several dams have been built on rivers and lakes to provide hydroelectric power throughout the country.

Danger from hurricanes, volcanoes, and earthquakes is always present in Costa Rica. These dangers, however, usually do not affect where people choose to live.

Human activity has had many negative effects on the environment in Costa Rica. Many forests have been destroyed. Land was often cleared for building homes and industries. Forest clearing was also done by the timber industry and for cattle ranches. Water pollution affects rivers and coastal waters. Pollution, along with loss of forests, threatens wildlife and plant life in Costa Rica.

Costa Rica, however, is known for its strong dedication to preserving its environment. The government has established national parks to protect the wildlife and plant life.

These beautiful areas as well as the pleasant climate have made Costa Rica a center for ecotourism.

Ecotourism is when people come to visit natural habitats that are preserved and seek to protect the environment while there. More than one million people visit Costa Rica each year.

Costa Rica's transportation system is made up of highways and railroads that enable its people to travel. Railroads connect the country from east to west, linking the port cities to the rest of the country. Buses, cars, and trucks move people and goods.

Costa Rica has several large and modern shipping ports. Limón, on the east coast, is the busiest port. From these ports, goods such as coffee, sugar, and bananas are shipped out of the country. The Inter-American Highway connects Costa Rica to the rest of Central America. Juan Santamaría is an important airport for international travel.

Costa Rica has eight daily newspapers. *La Nación* is the most popular of these. Costa Rica also has well over 70 radio stations and about six TV stations. Some Costa Rican writers, such as Fabián Dobles, have become known in other parts of the world for their work.

The Meseta Central is the center of Costa Rica's transportation system. From San José, buses go to most parts of the country.

Limón is the busiest port in Costa Rica.

Many Costa Ricans in the countryside often travel on horseback.

19

Costa Rica is part of both physical and cultural regions. Costa Rica is part of a cultural region called Latin America, where most people speak a Romance language, such as Spanish, Portuguese, or French. Latin America is made up of countries in the Western Hemisphere south of the United States, including the West Indies.

Costa Rica is part of many physical regions. It is part of the region known as Central America. Central America is made up of a long, narrow stretch of land that connects North America and South America. Costa Rica is also within the region known as the Ring of Fire, which goes around the Pacific Ocean. Many earthquakes and volcanoes occur in this region. In northern Costa Rica, the mountains of Cordillera Volcánia experience volcanic activity.

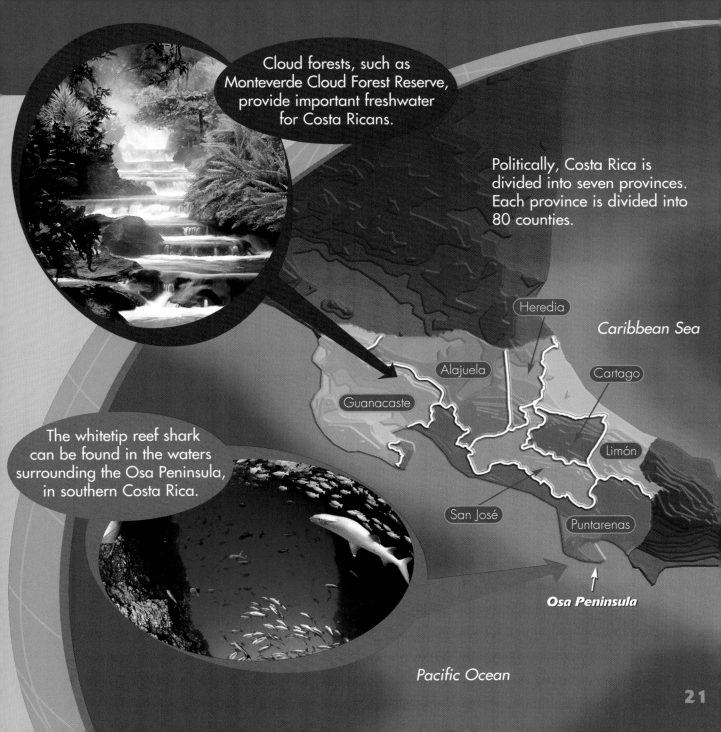

Cloud forests, such as Monteverde Cloud Forest Reserve, provide important freshwater for Costa Ricans.

Politically, Costa Rica is divided into seven provinces. Each province is divided into 80 counties.

The whitetip reef shark can be found in the waters surrounding the Osa Peninsula, in southern Costa Rica.

Heredia

Caribbean Sea

Alajuela

Cartago

Guanacaste

Limón

San José

Puntarenas

Osa Peninsula

Pacific Ocean

21

Costa Rica's Flag

Population (2003) 3,896,092

Language Spanish

Absolute location 10° north, 84° west

Capital city San José

Area 19,730 square miles (51,100 square kilometers)

Highest point Chirripó Grande 12,530 feet (3,819 meters)

Lowest point Pacific coast (zero feet)

Land boundaries Nicaragua and Panama

Natural resources fertile soil and hydroelectric power

Agricultural products avocados, coffee, mangoes, rice, sugarcane, tobacco, and cacao beans

Major exports bananas, beef, coffee, computer chips, and sugar

Major imports petroleum, chemicals, and manufactured goods

Glossary

culture (KUHL-chur) The way of life, ideas, customs, and traditions shared by a group of people.

fertile (FUR-tuhl) Able to grow plenty of plants.

habitat (HAB-uh-tat) The place and natural conditions where plants or animals live.

hydroelectric power (hye-droh-i-LEK-trik POU-ur) Water power that is used to turn a generator to produce electricity.

interaction (in-tur-AK-shuhn) The action between people, groups, or things.

plateau (pla-TOH) An area of high, flat land.

province (PROV-uhnss) A district or region of some countries.

region (REE-juhn) An area or a district.

republic (ri-PUHB-lik) A form of government in which the people have the power to elect representatives who manage the government.

resource (ri-SORSS) Something that is valuable or useful to a place or person.

volcano (vol-KA-noh) A mountain with an opening through which steam, ashes, and lava are sometimes forced out.

wetland (WET-land) Land where there is much moisture in the soil.

Index

Web Sites

Due to the changing nature of Internet links, PowerKids Press has developed an on-line list of Web sites related to the subject of this book. This site is updated regularly. Please use this link to access the list:
http://www.powerkidslinks.com/lwh/costa